Rosa Parks

7053

Samantha Bell

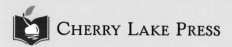
CHERRY LAKE PRESS

Published in the United States of America by Cherry Lake Publishing Group
Ann Arbor, Michigan
www.cherrylakepublishing.com

Reading Adviser: Beth Walker Gambro, MS, Ed., Reading Consultant, Yorkville, IL

Photo Credits: cover, page 17: © AP Photo/Montgomery County Sheriff's office; pages 5, 25: Library of Congress; page 6: © James Steidl/Shutterstock; page 7: © Gino Santa Maria/Shutterstock; page 8: Architect of the Capitol; page 9: © Sutherland Boswell/Shutterstock; page 11: Alvin C. Krupnick Co./Library of Congress; pages 12, 26–29: Rosa Parks Papers, Library of Congress; page 14: City of Montgomery, Alabama; page 15: Collection of the Smithsonian National Museum of African American History and Culture, Gift of Lauren and Michael Lee; page 16: Gene Herrick/Associated Press/National Portrait Gallery, Smithsonian Institution via Wikimedia Commons; pages 19, 20: Fellowship of Reconciliation via Comic Books Plus; page 21: Chronicling America: Historic American Newspapers, Library of Congress; page 22: Black Women Oral History Project, Schlesinger Library on the History of Women in America; page 23: © Anton_Ivanov/Shutterstock; page 30: © Olga Pylypenko/Shutterstock

Cherry Lake Press is an imprint of Cherry Lake Publishing Group.

Library of Congress Cataloging-in-Publication Data has been filed and is available at catalog.loc.gov.

Cherry Lake Publishing Group would like to acknowledge the work of the Partnership for 21st Century Learning, a Network of Battelle for Kids. Please visit http://www.battelleforkids.org/networks/p21 for more information.

Printed in the United States of America
Corporate Graphics

Note from publisher: Websites change regularly, and their future contents are outside of our control. Supervise children when conducting any recommended online searches for extended learning opportunities.

Samantha Bell was born and raised near Orlando, Florida. She grew up in a family of eight kids and all kinds of pets, including goats, chickens, cats, dogs, rabbits, horses, parakeets, hamsters, guinea pigs, a monkey, a raccoon, and a coatimundi. She now lives with her family in the foothills of the Blue Ridge Mountains, where she enjoys hiking, painting, and snuggling with their cats Pocket, Pebble, and Mr. Tree-Tree Triggers.

CONTENTS

CHAPTER 1

The Story People Tell

Too Tired to Stand

After the Civil War (1861–1865), slavery in the United States ended. But racial tensions were still running high. In the 1870s, Southern states began passing new laws. They were known as Jim Crow laws. They required White and Black people to remain separate in public places. These places included restaurants, theaters, stores, and restrooms. Black and White people were also separated on buses and trains. Generally, the places for White people were more comfortable than those for Black people. These laws were in effect for nearly 100 years.

This 1943 photo of the Greyhound bus station in Memphis, Tennessee, shows a Whites-only waiting room.

Black people and their allies worked for change throughout this time. This work turned into the civil rights movement. This movement made Jim Crow laws illegal. Leaders of the movement helped make this happen. Over time, some of their stories got **distorted**. This is what happened to the story of Rosa Parks. A fictional retelling was taught as fact.

In 1955, Rosa Parks worked as a **seamstress** in Montgomery, Alabama. She traveled by city bus to her job at a department store. Black and White people sat in different sections on the bus. White people had seats in the front. Black people had to sit in the back. Sometimes all of the seats were full when a White person got on. If that happened, a Black passenger would have to give them their seat.

Display of a Montgomery city bus at a Rosa Parks exhibit at the National Civil Rights Museum in Memphis, Tennessee

The story people tell says that one day Parks was coming home from work. It had been a long day, and she was very tired. She got on the bus, and soon every seat was full. Then a White man got on the bus. The bus driver told Parks to move. According to the law, she had to give her seat to him. But Parks was just too tired. She decided to stay seated.

The bus driver told Parks again, but she still refused. Finally, the bus driver called the police. A police officer came and arrested Rosa, and she went to jail. At the time, a Black reverend named Dr. Martin Luther King Jr. heard about what happened to Parks. He helped organize other Black residents in a **protest**. They decided to **boycott** the public buses. They did not ride the city buses for more than a year. This hurt the city's economy. It was a peaceful way to take a stand.

The story says that Parks's simple act of refusing to give up her seat started a movement. Black people began taking a stand against the unjust laws. Over time, the laws

AT THE CAPITOL

The U.S. Congress commissioned a statue of Rosa Parks in 2005. The statue is made of **bronze** and stands about 9 feet (2.7 meters) tall. It was completed in 2015. The statue is on display in Washington, D.C. It is the first full-length statue of a Black American in the U.S. Capitol. It depicts Parks the way she looked the day she was arrested. She is seated, symbolizing her refusal to give up her bus seat.

This statue of Rosa Parks was unveiled in 2019 in Montgomery, Alabama.

were changed. Black Americans began to enjoy the same freedoms as White Americans. Rosa Parks showed that the actions of just one individual can change the world. She became known as the "mother of the civil rights movement."

The facts of the matter show that Parks was already part of something much bigger. She didn't just stumble into the movement, too tired to stand. She was a fierce and determined freedom fighter long before she ever stepped on that Montgomery bus.

CHAPTER 2

The Facts of the Matter

Freedom Fighter

Jim Crow laws took away many freedoms and opportunities from Black Americans. But some White people prevented them from exercising their rights in other ways, too. Soon after the Civil War ended, some White people formed a secret organization called the Ku Klux Klan (KKK). The KKK used **intimidation** and violence to keep Black people from voting or even living life freely.

Rosa Louise McCauley was born on February 4, 1913, in Tuskegee, Alabama. She grew up in her grandparents' house in Pine Level, Alabama. She had to follow the Jim Crow laws. When she was a girl, the KKK was a constant threat. Her family had to board up the doors and windows of their home for safety. Sometimes Rosa stayed awake at night with her grandfather in case a KKK member tried to come inside. Living in fear became a way of life.

Racial violence was not just the work of the KKK. In 1921, a White mob burned over 35 blocks of a wealthy Black neighborhood in Tulsa, Oklahoma. The neighborhood was called Black Wall Street. Hundreds were killed and even more injured. Ten thousand people were left homeless.

Raymond Parks (second from left) was a barber in Montgomery, Alabama.

When she was 19, Rosa McCauley met Raymond Parks. He was the first real activist she knew. He was a member of the National Association for the Advancement of Colored People (NAACP). This group is the oldest U.S. civil rights organization. At the time, Raymond Parks was working to help some young Black men. They had been found guilty of a crime they did not commit. McCauley was proud of Raymond Parks's work. She also admired his courage.

Rosa McCauley married Raymond Parks and became an activist, too. Her married name was Rosa Parks. In 1943, Rosa Parks joined the NAACP and became the secretary of the Montgomery chapter. She also led the Montgomery NAACP Youth Council during this time.

Parks and her husband focused on voter registration, **desegregation**, and justice for Black people. She worked to help victims of violent crimes as well as people accused of crimes they did not commit. Rosa Parks helped bring national attention to crimes committed against Black people. She interviewed people and investigated where police departments wouldn't. In one instance, a sheriff even tried to scare her away. It didn't work.

In March 1955, Claudette Colvin was arrested for not giving up her seat on the bus. Claudette was 15 years old. She was a member of the Montgomery NAACP Youth Council. She had been learning about rights and freedoms in school. She knew that segregation laws were unfair. She chose to protest them.

A GROUP EFFORT

During the boycott, thousands of Black people who once rode the buses found other ways to get to work. Boycott leaders organized a **carpool**. Up to 325 people volunteered their cars. People figured out other ways to get to work. Some hitchhiked. Others walked. Some White housewives picked up their household workers and took them home again. Finally, in November 1956, the U.S. Supreme Court ruled segregation on public buses was unconstitutional. The case that changed the law was called *Browder v. Gayle*.

One month later, Aurelia Browder sat in the White section of the bus and refused to move. She was also arrested. In October, Mary Louise Smith was tired and frustrated. She was a housekeeper who went across town to collect her pay. Her clients weren't home. She was riding the bus home without her pay. A White man stood up to give a White woman his seat. He then wanted Smith to get up and give him her seat. She refused. He went and spoke with the driver. The bus driver told her to move. She refused. The bus driver pulled over and Smith was arrested.

Six days after Smith was arrested, another woman was as well. On October 21, Susan McDonald was arrested for not giving up her seat. McDonald was 77 years old. She was the widow of a United States veteran. McDonald was called "Mama Sue" or "Miss Sue" in the community. A fifth woman was also arrested. Her name was Jeanette Reese.

On December 1, 1955, 42-year-old Rosa Parks was working for Montgomery Fair department store. At the end of the day, she got onto a city bus in Montgomery, Alabama.

Mamie Till-Mobley (center) changed the direction of a nation by letting the world see her grief. She insisted on an open casket for her murdered son, Emmett Till. She wanted the world to see what the men had done to her son.

Just a few days before, she had learned that the men who killed 14-year-old Emmett Till, a young Black boy, would go free. She also knew that Black women kept being arrested. She was angry and frustrated by the lack of equal justice.

The first 10 seats were reserved for White people. Rosa Parks sat in the first row behind the 10 seats. Three other Black passengers also sat in her row. The bus became crowded, and more White passengers boarded. The bus driver told Parks and the other three Black passengers to move. The others moved, but Parks stayed seated. She was tired of being pushed around. She wasn't going to

Rosa Parks being fingerprinted by Deputy Sheriff D. H. Lackey after being arrested on February 22, 1956, during the Montgomery bus boycott, months after her first arrest in December for not giving up her seat.

take it anymore. She told the bus driver that she was not in a seat reserved for Whites. The bus driver called the police. Two officers came and arrested her.

Parks was not the first person to take a stand against the segregation laws on the city buses. But she was well respected by everyone who knew her. Her arrest brought the Black community together. They knew the arrests were wrong. They formed an organization to lead a boycott. They voted in a leader. The leader was the young pastor of the Dexter Avenue Baptist Church. His name was Martin Luther King Jr. He led Black residents in an organized protest. They boycotted the city buses on December 5, the day of Parks's trial. Ninety percent of the city's Black citizens stayed off the buses. The boycott worked so well that they decided to extend it. The boycott lasted 381 days.

The Black community didn't just boycott. They also filed a lawsuit on February 1, 1956. The lawsuit did not include Parks's arrest. It was still being processed in state courts. Instead, the lawsuit was for the arrests of Browder, Colvin, Smith, McDonald, and Reese. Jeanette Reese soon backed out. She and her husband faced threats and harassment. It was not safe for any of the plaintiffs.

Parks also paid for taking a stand. Both she and her husband lost their jobs. They never found steady work in Montgomery again, and they became very poor. They received many death threats. Eight months after the boycott ended, they moved to Detroit, Michigan, to live with family. They still struggled to find work and pay the bills. It took 11 years for Rosa to find a job that paid enough. But she continued to fight for freedom for many more years.

CHAPTER 3

Spinning the Story

Dignified but Determined

Rosa Parks was a brave, outspoken woman. She did not plan to start a large movement when she got on the bus that day. But she was not just a quiet, tired seamstress trying to get home. This view of Parks began with printed materials about her.

In 1957, a comic book was published to tell the story of Martin Luther King Jr. and Montgomery, Alabama. It was written to show what nonviolent protest could do. The story focuses on a young Black man. He is inspired by Parks's bravery and becomes an activist. The comic book was 16 pages long, and Parks is mentioned on one page. It shows the bus driver asking her to move. Parks quietly says no because she is tired and her feet ache. This became the picture many people had of Parks. The comic book was sent to churches, schools, and civil rights groups.

The cover of the 1957 comic book about the Montgomery bus boycott. At the time, *Negroes* was a term used for Black Americans.

Page 4 of the comic says Parks was tired and that her feet ached. It says she was not a trouble-maker.

Rosa Parks And Family Leave Montgomery, Ala.

Mrs. Rosa Parks, who set off the spark which put Montgomery, Ala., in the spotlight and resulted in the leadership of Dr. Martin Luther King, has left her home town for good. She and her husband Raymond A. Parks and her mother moved to Detroit, Mich., where they hope to find a quiter and more secure life.

Mrs. Parks, whose work as a talented seamstress, had fallen off considerably; says that she cannot really say that the "reaction from what happened in the boycott made us leave. We really had been thinking about it for a long time and I guess some things do have a way of helping you decide."

The Parks will live at 449 East Euclid, Detroit, Mich.

INTERRACIAL ALL-STAR BASEBALL AT SALEM STADIUM AUGUST 31

Baseball fans are in for a sensational ball game at Salem Municipal Stadium Saturday night, August 31. The Maryland All-Stars of Baltimore, Md., will tangle with the Virginia Mountain All-Star League (white), in one of the season's most sensational games. The Maryland All-Stars will feature the one-arm king of baseball. His one-arm home run batting in a recent game at the Salem Stadium is still the talk of the town.

The game will start promptly at 8:00 p.m. Don't miss this game of the season.

This clip is from the Roanoke, Virginia, newspaper the *Tribune*. The article ran in the August 24, 1957, issue.

Newspapers reported on Parks's move from Montgomery to Detroit. But even Black newspapers softened the reports. They did not describe the death threats and poverty the Parks family endured in Montgomery. For example, an article in the *Tribune* in Roanoke, Virginia, told about the move. But it stated only that Rosa's family was looking for a quieter, more secure life.

Ten years after Rosa's arrest, a Los Angeles newspaper ran an article about her. In the article, she was described as an everyday woman on a bus. The article said Rosa was quiet, **pious**, and dignified. She did not think about being famous. According to the article, that would have been unladylike.

Today, many children are still taught just a small part of Rosa's story. Picture books and biographies usually show her as the gentle seamstress with tired feet. Books that discuss other parts of her life often focus more on her

STILL MISTAKEN

When Rosa died in 2005, obituaries and tributes to her appeared in many newspapers and online. Some of these still described her incorrectly. For example, in the **obituary** issued by the funeral home, Rosa was described as "the quiet seamstress who sparked the desegregation movement." There is no mention of her work as a civil rights activist.

A wax figure of Rosa Parks on display in San Francisco portrays her in later years. Many versions of her story incorrectly describe Parks as an old woman instead of the 42-year-old she was.

character. They leave out her political views. But these views affected the decisions she made throughout her life. Rosa Parks was not brave only during that moment on the bus. She showed courage all through the years before and

CHAPTER 4

Writing History

Evaluating Sources

One of the best ways to learn about a historical event is from someone who experienced it. People can find out about Rosa Parks and the Montgomery bus boycott from Parks herself. In 1992, Rosa published an **autobiography**, *My Story.* The book tells the story of her life from her point of view. It begins with her childhood. It covers events in her life through 1989.

When a person writes an autobiography, they do more than just write facts about historical events. They also write about how the events affected them. They talk about how they felt at the time. For example, Parks mentions an argument she had with a White boy. Parks was about 10 years old. She and the boy were on the same road. The boy threatened to hit her. She picked up a brick and dared him to try. The boy changed his mind and left. Parks's grandmother **scolded** her. She thought Parks would get in trouble. But Parks thought she was right to defend herself.

Parks speaks at the Poor People's March at Washington Monument and Lincoln Memorial in June 1968.

Parks visited many schools and classrooms like this. Many students sent her cards and letters after learning about her in class.

Other sources for learning about Rosa Parks are now available. In 2015, a collection of Parks's photographs and writings were shared with the public. These documents are known as the Rosa Parks Collection. They are located at the Library of Congress in Washington, D.C. Some of the papers are very personal. They include letters to her mother and her husband, Raymond Parks. There is a recipe for pancakes with peanut butter. The collection also includes her Bible and prayers she wrote down. These documents provide a special glimpse into Parks's life.

The collection also includes many documents about the fight for civil rights. These include speech notes and political documents. One document is a receipt for $1.50 for a poll tax. Voting is a right of all Americans. But because of the Jim Crow laws, Parks and other Black citizens had to pay a tax to vote. The collection also includes her thoughts about the struggle of Black Americans. She told about the crimes against them by White people and the lack of justice. She wrote about the disappointment, hurt, and oppression they suffered.

A LIFETIME IN PICTURES

The Rosa Parks Collection includes 2,500 photos. They show both her personal life and her work as an activist. Some are photos of the house where she was born. There are also photos of her husband. One shows Parks and her husband at an NAACP dinner together. Another is a wallet-size photo of Raymond Parks that she carried with her.

May 19, 1956

Dear Mother:

This leaves my doing fine. I have had quite a stay here in New York. I was very glad to receive the letters and clippings from you. The people here are very nice. I spent Thursday night with Mr + Mrs. Thurgood Marshall. So much is going on I can't tell it in this letter. It will have to wait till I get home. I am accepting the Washington, D.C invitation and will be home right afterward.

I will stay here for the Madison Square Garden Rally May 24. I hope you and Parks are making out all right. I am not staying with the Meachams now,

Rosa Parks toured the country in 1956 speaking about the bus boycott. In this letter to her mother in May, she talks about having dinner with Thurgood Marshall. Eleven years later, Marshall became the first Black Supreme Court Justice.

She wrote on anything she had at the time, including envelopes, church programs, and notebook pages. Some pieces are about the bus in Montgomery. In one of them, she writes about how she had been pushed around all her life. At that moment, she could not take it anymore.

The collection includes 7,500 manuscripts. These personal papers and keepsakes contain a much richer story of Rosa Parks. They provide a record of events in her life as she was experiencing them. They reveal that she was a courageous woman from the start.

Activity
Letters to Home

The Rosa Parks Collection contains many personal letters she wrote to friends and family. They don't tell only what was going on in her life. They also tell how she felt about it. Write your own letter to a friend or family member. Describe something that is happening in your life or in the world around you right now. Share your thoughts and feelings. What do you want your friend or family member to understand most?

Learn More

Books

Baptiste, Tracey, and Shauna J. Grant. *Rosa Parks & Claudette Colvin: Civil Rights Heroes.* New York, NY: First Second Books, 2023.

Burke, Laura. *It's Her Story: Rosa Parks.* Chicago, IL: Sunbird Books, 2021.

Fitzpatrick, Insha. *Who Sparked the Montgomery Bus Boycott?: Rosa Parks.* New York, NY: Penguin Workshop, 2021.

Parks, Rosa, and Jim Haskins. *Rosa Parks: My Story.* New York, NY: Puffin Books, 1999.

On the Web

With an adult, explore more online with these suggested searches.

"Rosa Parks Was Arrested for Civil Disobedience," America's Library

"The Life of Rosa Parks," National Geographic Kids

The United States Civil Rights Trail

"This is Rosa: Read the Story of Rosa Parks," Time for Kids

Glossary

autobiography (ah-toh-bye-AH-gruh-fee) the story of someone's life written by that person

boycott (BOY-kaht) to refuse to buy or use something or go into a certain place in order to bring about a change

bronze (BRAHNZ) a mixture of copper and tin

carpool (KAHR-poohl) an agreement among a group of people to make a regular journey in a car together, usually with each person taking turns driving

desegregation (dee-seh-grih-GAY-shuhn) ending a policy of separating people by race

distorted (dih-STOR-tuhd) warped or changed from a true condition

intimidation (in-tih-muh-DAY-shuhn) the act of making another fearful by means of threats or other shows of power

obituary (oh-BIH-chuh-wair-ee) a notice of death, often published in a newspaper

pious (PYE-uhss) showing love for God; religious

plaintiffs (PLAYN-tuhfs) people who ask the court to rule on a legal matter

protest (PROH-test) an expression of being against something

scolded (SKOLDED) spoke in a sharp or angry way

seamstress (SEEM-struhss) a woman who sews as her occupation

Index